JOURNEY CHRISTIANE AMANPOUR BIOGRAPHY

By
Barbara M. Cook

All rights reserved © 2024 Barbara M. Cook

The scanning, uploading, and dissemination of this work online or by any other means without the author's written consent is prohibited and unlawful, unless allowed by the U.S. Copyright Act of 1976. Please do not engage in or promote the electronic piracy of protected content; instead, only buy authorized paperback and electronic versions. The purpose of this publication is to offer knowledgeable and trustworthy information on the topics discussed.

DISCLAIMER

This book contains material that is intended solely for informative purposes.

ABOUT THE AUTHOR

The author of this biography, Barbara, is an experienced journalist and writer with a passion for storytelling and a dedication to capturing the spirit of amazing people. With a history in journalism and a great respect for the power of storytelling, Barbara brings a lot of expertise and insight to the mission of documenting Christiane Amanpour's life and legacy.

Barbara has worked in numerous capacities in the world of journalism and understands firsthand the struggles and achievements that define the lives of individuals who commit themselves to the quest for truth and justice. Drawing from this rich tapestry of experiences, Barbara approaches biography writing with a strong eye for detail, a respect for accuracy, and a commitment to capture the soul of its subject.

In writing this biography of Christiane Amanpour, Barbara hopes to not only expose the astounding achievements of one of the world's greatest journalists but also to urge readers to consider the power of narrative to alter our perception of the world and our role in it. Through rigorous research, insightful thinking, and entertaining storytelling, Barbara takes readers on a journey through the life and legacy of an amazing person.

As an author, Barbara is dedicated to giving readers a nuanced and informative image of Christiane Amanpour, one that celebrates her accomplishments while also addressing the complexity of her life and work. Barbara hopes that this biography will not only enlighten and delight readers, but also encourage them to embrace the principles of integrity, courage, and empathy that are central to Christiane Amanpour's incredible journey.

PREFACE

In the ever-changing environment of media, certain voices go beyond basic reporting, affecting the fundamental fabric of our knowledge and empathy. Christiane Amanpour is a towering figure in her field, with a decades-long career distinguished by an unshakable commitment to truth, the daring pursuit of stories from the front lines, and impassioned advocacy for the voiceless.

This preamble is an homage to her incredible path, which is marked by courage, honesty, and compassion. From her early days as a war correspondent to her current position as a leading voice in global journalism, Christiane has not only reported the news, but also illuminated the human stories behind the headlines, amplifying the voices of those who are frequently silenced by conflict, oppression, and injustice.

As we read on, we will take a trip through Christiane Amanpour's life and legacy, celebrating journalism's ability to enlighten, inspire, and ignite change. Christiane Amanpour has made an indelible impression on the world of media and beyond with her unequaled devotion to truth, relentless support for press freedom and human rights, and unflinching confidence in the power of narrative to transcend divisions and build understanding.

Table of Contents

DISCLAIMER 3
ABOUT THE AUTHOR 4
PREFACE 6
INTRODUCTION 11
Chapter 1 14
   PURPOSE OF THE BIOGRAPHY 14
Chapter 2 16
   Early Life and Background 16
CHILDHOOD INFLUENCES AND EDUCATION 19
Chapter 3 24
   Career Beginnings 24
MILESTONES AND CHALLENGES 30
Chapter 4 34
   Rise to Prominence 34
NOTABLE REPORTING ASSIGNMENTS 37
RECOGNITION AND AWARDS 40
Chapter 5 43
   Reporting Style and Philosophy 43
REPORTING IN CONFLICT ZONES 47
Chapter 6 50
   Personal Life and Challenges 50
IMPACT ON RELATIONSHIP AND FAMILY 53
PERSONAL CHALLENGES AND RESILIENCE 56
Chapter 7 60
   Amanpour's Global Influence 60

LEGACY AND INFLUENCE ON JOURNALISM 64

Chapter 8 68

    Criticism and Controversies 68

Chapter 9 72

    BEYOND JOURNALISM 72

CONCLUSION 76

INTRODUCTION

Few names stand out more in the ever-changing fabric of modern journalism than Christiane Amanpour's. With her typical fearlessness, unshakable devotion to truth, and dogged pursuit of important issues, Amanpour has established herself as a light of honesty and intelligence in international reporting.

Amanpour was born on January 12, 1958, in London, England, to an Iranian father and a British mother. Her eclectic background helped shape her global perspective and strong empathy for the human condition. She was endowed with a curiosity about the world outside her boundaries from birth, which would push her on a remarkable voyage across the turbulent landscapes of international conflict and diplomacy.

Amanpour's rise to journalistic fame was the result of sheer dedication and guts, not luxury or coincidence. With a bachelor's degree in journalism and a master's degree in journalism from the University of Rhode Island, she began her work with a strong desire to bear witness to history and give voice to the voiceless.

Her ascension through the ranks of journalism was rapid. From her early days as a desk assistant at CNN to her key role as the network's senior international correspondent, Amanpour soon established a reputation for courageous reporting from the front lines of combat zones and insightful conversations with global leaders.

But, despite the honors and adulation, what truly distinguishes Amanpour is her unrelenting dedication to the ideals of truth and honesty in journalism. In an age of sensationalism and soundbites, she is a staunch supporter of careful fact-checking, nuanced analysis, and the power of narrative to bridge gaps and encourage understanding.

Throughout her remarkable career, Amanpour has not only shed light on the world's dark corners but has also encouraged numerous young journalists to follow her lead. Her commitment to speaking truth to power, compassion for the suffering of others, and unwavering trust in journalism's ability to influence positive change serve as a beacon for all of us.

As we start on this journey through Christiane Amanpour's life and legacy, let us not only celebrate her incredible accomplishments but also reflect on the ongoing role of journalism in influencing the society we live in and want to create.

Chapter 1

PURPOSE OF THE BIOGRAPHY

The goal of this biography is to provide readers with a thorough insight into Christiane Amanpour's life, career, and impact, as one of today's most prominent journalists. This biography tries to explore Amanpour's path in detail.

Educate and Inform: By charting Amanpour's life from childhood to her trailblazing journalism, the biography aims to educate readers about the key events and milestones that have defined her career.

Inspire and Motivate: Amanpour's narrative exemplifies tenacity, courage, and resilience. Her uncompromising devotion to truth and justice has inspired many people all around the world. This biography seeks to inspire readers by showcasing Amanpour's accomplishments and the hardships she has faced.

Provide Insight and Analysis: In addition to detailing Amanpour's successes, the biography dives into the larger context of her work, exploring the ethical quandaries she has encountered, the impact of her reporting on global events, and her influence on the world of journalism.

Celebrate a Trailblazer: Amanpour's achievements in journalism, notably her reporting from crisis zones and dedication to giving voice to the voiceless have garnered her global respect and appreciation. This biography honors her as a trailblazer who has set the standard for future generations of journalists.

Encourage Reflection and Dialogue: By delving deeply into Amanpour's life and impact, the biography challenges readers to consider the role of journalism in society, the significance of maintaining journalistic integrity, and the power of narrative to affect good change.

Chapter 2

Early Life and Background

BIRTH AND FAMILY BACKGROUND

Christiane Amanpour was born on January 12, 1958, in London, England, to a family of mixed ethnicity. Her father, Mohammad Taghi Amanpour, was Iranian, while her mother, Patricia Anne Hill, was British. This unusual cultural combination would subsequently influence Christiane's outlook and journalistic viewpoint.

Christiane was up in a cosmopolitan setting, inspired by both her Iranian and British heritage. Her parents' different origins gave her a broad tapestry of experiences and viewpoints from a young age.

Despite her cosmopolitan background, Christiane's childhood was not without difficulties. Her family was uprooted and displaced as a result of political unrest in Iran, forcing them to migrate to England when she was a small kid. These early experiences with instability and adaptability would eventually shape Christiane's reporting on worldwide wars and humanitarian catastrophes.

Christiane's family encouraged her to follow her passions and interests. Both of her parents encouraged education and intellectual curiosity, fostering in her a passion for learning and a hunger for information. It was this intellectual stimulation and encouragement that eventually led Christiane to a career in journalism.

As Christiane's profession progressed, her family provided strength and support. Despite the pressures of her job as an international journalist, she remained close to her family and frequently credited them with defining her ideals and helping her through life's trials.

In narrating her path from a multicultural background to becoming one of the world's most renowned journalists, Christiane frequently comments on her family's impact and the lessons they taught her. Their love, perseverance, and unflinching confidence in the power of truth have inspired her throughout her career, helping to shape her into the strong journalist and human rights campaigner she is today.

CHILDHOOD INFLUENCES AND EDUCATION

Christiane Amanpour's early years were characterized by a mix of cultural influences and a desire to learn, which would determine her future career as a journalist.

Growing up in a multicultural environment in London, England, Christiane was exposed to a wide range of opinions from a young age. Her Iranian father and British mother instilled in her a strong awareness of many cultures, languages, and ways of thinking. This upbringing created in Christiane a genuine interest in the world outside her immediate surroundings, laying the groundwork for her future profession as a travel journalist.

Throughout her childhood, Christiane had a ravenous hunger for knowledge. She was a bright student who excelled intellectually, driven by a desire to grasp the complexity of the world around her. Her parents recognized her intellectual curiosity and encouraged her to follow her hobbies while also providing her with the necessary support and resources to succeed.

Christiane's interest in storytelling and current affairs grew throughout her studies. She devoured newspapers and novels, immersing herself in stories of foreign nations and battles. During these formative years, Christiane began to consider a career in journalism, realizing the power of narrative to expose injustice and promote change.

After finishing her secondary school, Christiane attended the University of Rhode Island and received a bachelor's degree in journalism. Her academic experience gave her a firm foundation in journalistic concepts as well as the abilities she needed to excel in the industry.

Undeterred by the hurdles of getting into the competitive world of media, Christiane continued her studies by earning a master's degree in journalism from the University of Rhode Island. Armed with academic qualifications and a strong desire to make a difference, she began her work with a feeling of purpose and resolve.

Christiane Amanpour's life and career have been influenced by important cultural and historical events that have left a lasting impact.

Born in 1958, Christiane grew up amid a time of global turmoil and transition. Cold War tensions between the United States and the Soviet Union loomed over global affairs, impacting international relations and conflicts all across the world. Growing up in London, Christiane was acutely aware of the geopolitical dynamics of the time, as well as the social and cultural upheavals taking place both at home and abroad.

The 1979 Iranian Revolution, which witnessed the removal of the Shah and the foundation of an Islamic Republic, had a significant influence on Christiane's life and personality. As the daughter of an Iranian father, she witnessed directly the consequences of this seismic catastrophe, which caused political turmoil and social transformation in Iran and rippled across the region and beyond. This time of instability and uncertainty would subsequently influence Christiane's reporting on Middle Eastern issues and her awareness of the region's intricacies.

Against the backdrop of global turmoil, Christiane continued her schooling and began her career in journalism. She began her career as a journalist in the 1980s and 1990s, at a period of fast global change. The fall of the Soviet Union, the end of apartheid in South Africa, and the appearance of new wars and humanitarian crises all transformed the global scene, presenting journalists like Christiane with new difficulties and opportunities.

Christiane has bravely and compassionately covered conflicts, revolutions, and humanitarian crises around the globe. Her reportage has shed light on the human cost of violence and the plight of regular people caught in the crossfire. In doing so, she has not only witnessed history but also contributed to shaping the narrative of our day, shedding light on the intricacies of modern life and questioning conventional thought.

Chapter 3

Career Beginnings

ENTRY INTO JOURNALISM

Christiane Amanpour's path to journalism was distinguished by a mix of passion, determination, and dedication to elevating the voices of the disadvantaged and downtrodden.

Christiane had a strong interest in narrative and current events from a young age, which she attributed to her innate curiosity about her surroundings. This desire to comprehend the human experience and give witness to history would eventually push her to pursue a career in journalism.

Christiane set out on her professional career with a feeling of purpose and passion after graduating from the University of Rhode Island with a bachelor's and master's degree in journalism. Her academic background equipped her with a strong foundation in journalistic principles as well as the abilities required to negotiate the fast-paced and competitive world of news reporting.

Christiane sharpened her journalism skills in the early phases of her career through internships and entry-level roles, where she got vital hands-on experience and established her voice and style. She displayed a talent for identifying intriguing stories as well as a fearlessness in seeking the truth, both of which would become characteristics of her reporting in the years that followed.

Christiane's career took off while she worked at CNN. When she was hired as a desk assistant at the network's Atlanta headquarters, she rapidly made a name for herself with her remarkable work ethic, acute intelligence, and unshakable dedication to journalistic ethics. Her talent and determination piqued the interest of senior executives, who saw her potential and quickly elevated her to an on-air journalist.

As Christiane's career progressed at CNN, she established herself as one of the network's most regarded journalists, receiving accolades for her brave reporting from crisis zones and insightful conversations with global leaders. Her ability to shine a light on the human stories behind the headlines and give voice to the voiceless earned her reputation as an exceptional journalist with unrivaled skill and ethics.

EARLY WORK EXPERIENCE AND INFLUENCES

Christiane Amanpour's early job experience, as well as the influences that formed her formative years, had a huge impact on her path to becoming a journalist of exceptional courage and integrity.

As a young journalist, Christiane began her career with a thirst for information and a strong desire to create stories. Her academic education in journalism, along with her natural interest in the world, gave her a solid basis when she entered the business.

Christiane's early career was heavily influenced by her tenure as a desk assistant at CNN's Atlanta headquarters. This entry-level role introduced her to the inner workings of a worldwide news organization, giving her significant insight into the fast-paced and demanding world of broadcast journalism.

Christiane had the opportunity to work with seasoned journalists and industry veterans who acted as mentors and role models for her while at CNN. Their advice and support helped define Christiane's reporting style, instilling in her a dedication to accuracy, impartiality, and journalistic integrity that would become the hallmark of her work.

As her career advanced, Christiane welcomed opportunities to report from some of the world's most turbulent locations, such as the Balkans, the Middle East, and Africa. These experiences exposed her to the brutal realities of war, conflict, and humanitarian crises, while also expanding her knowledge of the human cost of violence and injustice.

Throughout her early career, Christiane was impacted by a wide range of voices and opinions, from fellow journalists and coworkers to people she met in the field. Their tales and difficulties motivated her to step up her efforts to give voice to the voiceless and bring attention to injustices and disparities that go unrecognized far too frequently.

MILESTONES AND CHALLENGES

Christiane Amanpour's career has been marked by several notable milestones and obstacles, each of which has influenced her development as a journalist and fighter for truth and justice.

Early Career Breakthroughs: Christiane's journey from desk assistant to CNN on-air journalist was one of her first major accomplishments. This was the start of her journey to popularity inside the network, giving her a platform to demonstrate her ability and passion for journalism.

Reporting from Conflict Zones: Throughout her career, Christiane has established herself as a daring reporter ready to travel to some of the world's most dangerous and unpredictable locations. Her coverage of crises in Bosnia,

Rwanda, Iraq, and Syria has gained her worldwide praise and proved her dedication to documenting the human cost of war.

Interviews with international Leaders: Christiane's insightful interviews with international leaders have also marked a watershed moment in her career. From presidents to dictators, she has held powerful persons accountable while also providing audiences with essential insights into the thoughts and motives of those who create world events.

Christiane has received several prizes and accolades for her services to journalism, including multiple Emmy prizes, the Edward R. Murrow Award for Excellence in Journalism, and the International Women's Media Foundation's Courage in Journalism Award. These distinctions demonstrate her impact and influence on the business.

obstacles and Controversies: Despite her numerous accomplishments, Christiane has experienced her fair share of obstacles and controversies during her career. From criticism of her reporting style to accusations of bias, she has weathered the storm with grace and bravery, emerging stronger and more determined to maintain the values of journalistic honesty and independence.

Balancing Personal and Professional Life: Christiane, like many journalists, has struggled to strike a balance between her hard job and her personal life. The pressures of reporting from combat zones, as well as bearing witness to human misery, have taken a toll on her personal life, forcing her to strike a careful balance between her professional commitments and her well-being.

Chapter 4

Rise to Prominence

Breakthrough Moments

Christiane Amanpour's career has been distinguished by multiple watershed moments that not only catapulted her to international prominence but also transformed the landscape of journalism.

Assignment to the Gulf War (1990-1991): Christiane's first big break came during the Gulf War when she distinguished herself as a brave reporter reporting from the front lines. Her coverage of the battle drew international attention and cemented her image as a journalist willing to go into dangerous situations to deliver viewers the truth.

Bosnian War Reporting (1992–1995): Christiane's reporting from the Bosnian War is seen as a watershed event in her career. Her heartbreaking stories of atrocities perpetrated throughout the conflict drew public attention to the suffering of civilians caught in the crossfire and played an important role in rallying global support for humanitarian assistance.

Exclusive Interviews with World Leaders: Throughout her career, Christiane has scored exclusive interviews with some of the world's most powerful figures, including presidents, prime ministers, and dictators. These interviews have given viewers unprecedented insights into the brains and motives of individuals who affect world events, while also cementing Christiane's position as one of the most renowned journalists in the industry.

Amanpour & Company (2018): In 2018, Christiane debuted "Amanpour & Company," a new late-night news program on PBS that goes beyond CNN. The show includes in-depth interviews with newsmakers and specialists on a variety of themes, reinforcing Christiane's reputation as a prominent voice in journalism.

Christiane's support for press freedom and human rights has been a distinguishing feature of her career. From speaking out against censorship and repression to advocating for the rights of journalists throughout the world, she has utilized her position to bring attention to topics that are sometimes neglected or disregarded.

NOTABLE REPORTING ASSIGNMENTS

Throughout her lengthy career, Christiane Amanpour has taken on various major reporting assignments, covering some of the most significant events and conflicts of the day. Here are some of her outstanding assignments:

Gulf War (1990-1991): Christiane grew to popularity for her brave reporting from the front lines of the Gulf War, offering viewers personal descriptions of the fighting and its consequences for the area. Her reporting gained her worldwide accolades and cemented her reputation as a fearless journalist willing to walk into dangerous situations.

Bosnian War (1992-1995): Christiane's reportage from the conflict drew public attention to the atrocities perpetrated and helped galvanize support for humanitarian intervention. Her heartbreaking stories of the misery faced by people caught in the crossfire influenced worldwide perceptions of the conflict and helped to advance peace efforts.

Rwandan Genocide (1994): Christiane wrote extensively on the Rwandan Genocide, sharing eyewitness reports of the horrors taking place in the country and the international community's refusal to assist. Her reportage put light on the scope of the crimes and contributed to raising awareness of the critical need for action to avert future loss of life.

Iraq War (2003): During the Iraq War, Christiane reported from the front lines, providing viewers with insights into the conflict's human cost as well as the intricacies of the ground situation. Her conversations with Iraqi residents, troops, and authorities presented a nuanced account of the conflict and its effects on the Iraqi people.

Arab Spring (2010-2012): Christiane covered the Arab Spring revolutions in the Middle East and

North Africa, giving viewers a front-row seat to history as popular rallies deposed despotic rulers and encouraged hope for democratic change. Her work provides essential insights into the social, political, and economic causes motivating the turmoil, as well as the obstacles to the region's democratic transition.

Syrian Civil War (2011-present): Christiane's coverage of the Syrian Civil War has been broad and compelling, providing viewers with insight into the conflict's catastrophic impact on people as well as the intricacies of the geopolitical processes at play. Her interviews with Syrian refugees, activists, and government officials have offered critical insights into the human tales behind the headlines, influencing global perceptions of the situation.

RECOGNITION AND AWARDS

Throughout her remarkable career, Christiane Amanpour has received several prizes and distinctions in recognition of her outstanding contributions to journalism and unshakable dedication to truth and ethics. Some of the most prominent recognitions are:

Emmy Awards: Christiane has received several Emmy Awards for her great reporting and coverage of major global events. Her Emmy awards include Outstanding Live Coverage of a Current News Story and Outstanding Interview.

Edward R. Murrow Award: She has received the Edward R. Murrow Award for Excellence in Journalism, which recognizes her outstanding work as an overseas reporter as well as her commitment to sustaining the highest journalistic ethics and professionalism.

Christiane got a Peabody Award, one of broadcasting's most prestigious distinctions, for her coverage of the Rwandan genocide. The Peabody Award acknowledged her work for its depth and effect, shedding attention to the atrocities occurring in the country and the urgent need for international assistance.

The International Women's Media Foundation presented Christiane with the Courage in Journalism Award in appreciation of her bravery and perseverance while reporting from conflict zones and difficult situations. This award recognizes her unflinching dedication to speaking truth to power and providing a voice for the voiceless.

Honorary Degrees: Christiane has received honorary degrees from various major universities in appreciation of her great contributions to journalism and her position as a global leader in the industry. These honorary degrees confirm her reputation as a renowned and prominent figure in the field of media and communication.

She has also received the Freedom of Speech Award from groups devoted to promoting press freedom and protecting journalists' rights. This award honors Christiane's gutsy advocacy for free expression and her unwavering dedication to holding authority accountable.

Chapter 5

Reporting Style and Philosophy

JOURNALISTIC APPROACHES AND ETHICS

Christiane Amanpour's journalistic approach is distinguished by her unwavering dedication to truth, honesty, and humanity. Throughout her career, she has followed a set of ethical standards that govern her reporting and influence her interactions with sources, topics, and viewers. Some important elements of her journalistic methodology and ethics include:

Seeking Truth: Christiane stresses the pursuit of truth over all else in her reporting. She undertakes extensive research, meticulously checks facts, and corroborates material from many sources to guarantee that her reports are accurate and reliable.

Objectivity and Impartiality: Christiane recognizes the necessity of objectivity and impartiality in journalism, but she also accepts the intrinsic subjectivity of human experience. She attempts to provide a balanced view in her reporting, giving voice to all sides of a topic while staying aware of her prejudices and assumptions.

Christiane approaches her work with a strong feeling of empathy and sympathy for the people whose tales she covers. She attempts to comprehend the human consequences of events and conflicts, acknowledging the dignity and humanity of individuals impacted by tragedy and injustice.

Independence and Autonomy: Christiane appreciates her journalistic independence and aggressively protects her right to pursue important topics. She is not tied to any political or corporate interests, and her reporting remains editorially independent.

Ethical Dilemmas and Decision-Making: When facing ethical quandaries, Christiane carefully evaluates the potential ramifications of her actions and attempts to minimize harm while preserving the public's right to know. When faced with tough issues, she interacts with coworkers, editors, and legal experts while adhering to the greatest journalistic ethics and professionalism.

Christiane thinks that openness and accountability are vital components of ethical journalism. She is honest about her methods and procedures, welcomes input and criticism from her audience and peers, and accepts responsibility for any errors or inaccuracies in her coverage.

Advocacy for Press Freedom: Christiane is a firm supporter of press freedom, defending journalists' rights to report freely and without fear of censorship or retaliation. She stands out against threats to press freedom and backs policies that safeguard journalists and promote a free and independent media.

REPORTING IN CONFLICT ZONES

Christiane Amanpour's reporting from crisis zones is distinguished by her unrivaled courage, sensitivity, and dedication to giving voice to the voiceless. Throughout her career, she has been to some of the world's most hazardous and volatile locations to shed light on the human cost of conflict and give testimony to the plight of people caught in the middle. Here are some important characteristics of her approach to reporting in crisis zones.

Courage Under Fire: Christiane's reporting from war zones frequently involves extreme danger and personal risk. Despite the inherent hazards, she is unwavering in her quest to offer viewers the truth from the front lines of conflict. Her bravery in the face of adversity has garnered her the affection and esteem of both colleagues and viewers.

Empathetic Storytelling: Christiane approaches her reporting with strong empathy and sympathy for the people whose lives are affected by war. She listens to their experiences with an open heart, eager to bear witness to their anguish and suffering. Her compassionate narrative humanizes war victims, fostering deeper understanding and empathy in viewers.

Balancing Objectivity and Advocacy: While being committed to objectivity and fairness, Christiane realizes the importance of advocacy when reporting from crisis zones. She utilizes her position to raise the voices of individuals who are frequently forgotten or disadvantaged, campaigning for their rights and highlighting the injustices they experience.

Navigating Ethical Dilemmas: Reporting from crisis zones frequently exposes journalists to challenging ethical quandaries. Christiane skillfully navigates these obstacles, balancing the risks and repercussions of her work while adhering to journalistic ethics and professionalism. When faced with tough issues, she works with coworkers, editors, and legal consultants, aiming to minimize harm while protecting the public's right to know.

raise Awareness: Christiane's reporting from conflict zones contributes significantly to raising awareness of the human cost of war and the urgent necessity for international engagement. Her tales provide audiences with a personal look at the reality of living in war-torn areas, exposing myths and encouraging action to address the core causes of violence and promote peace.

Chapter 6

Personal Life and Challenges

Balancing Personal and Professional Life

For Christiane Amanpour, managing her personal and professional lives has been a never-ending path of introspection, prioritizing, and self-care. Despite the demands of her job as an international reporter, she has walked the fine line between her professional obligations and her well-being with elegance and tenacity. Here are a few significant tactics she uses to preserve equilibrium:

Setting Boundaries: Christiane understands the significance of establishing clear boundaries between her job and home life. She sets apart certain hours for work and pleasure, allowing her to rest and reconnect with loved ones.

Prioritizing Self-Care: Despite the frantic speed of her profession, Christiane views self-care as an essential component of her routine. She devotes time to things that feed her body, mind, and soul, such as physical exercise, mindfulness and meditation, and hobbies and interests outside of work.

Seeking Support: Christiane relies on her family, friends, and coworkers for emotional support and encouragement. She cultivates genuine relationships with others who encourage and inspire her, giving her strength and perseverance during difficult times.

Embracing Flexibility: Recognizing the unexpected nature of her job as a writer, Christiane values flexibility and adaptation in her personal life. She stays adaptable and willing to amend her plans as necessary, allowing for spontaneity and serendipity to enrich her experiences.

Maintaining Perspective: Christiane keeps a healthy perspective on the significance of work-life balance, understanding that her personal happiness and well-being are critical for long-term success and fulfillment in her job. She confronts problems with perseverance and optimism, certain that she can overcome hurdles and prosper in all facets of her life.

IMPACT ON RELATIONSHIP AND FAMILY

Christiane Amanpour's successful work as an international journalist has surely had a significant influence on her personal and familial life. Christiane has faced both obstacles and possibilities as she balances the demands of high-pressure work with personal obligations and family duties. Here are some ways that her job has affected her relationships and family dynamics:

Time Away from Loved Ones: Christiane's frequent travel and assignments in war zones sometimes entail lengthy periods of absence from home, resulting in extensive time apart from her loved ones. This isolation can strain relationships and make it difficult to keep in contact with family and friends.

Emotional Toll: Reporting from combat zones and witnessing human suffering may be emotionally taxing for journalists like Christiane, compromising their mental health and well-being. The stress and trauma involved with her employment may impair her capacity to be completely present in her relationships and communicate meaningfully with loved ones.

Despite the difficulties of her job, Christiane is lucky to have a supporting network of family, friends, and coworkers who understand her work and provide constant support and encouragement. Their love and understanding give Christiane strength and perseverance in tough circumstances.

Shared Values and Priorities: Christiane's boyfriend and family members share her enthusiasm for journalism and desire to make a good difference in the world. They recognize the significance of her profession and the sacrifices she makes to follow her passion, which fosters a feeling of family togetherness and shared purpose.

Quality Time Together: When Christiane is not on assignment, she values the opportunity to spend quality time with her loved ones, making lasting memories and strengthening ties. Whether it's savoring leisurely dinners, participating in outdoor activities, or simply resting at home, she loves these times of connection and closeness with her family.

PERSONAL CHALLENGES AND RESILIENCE

Christiane Amanpour's career as a journalist has been defined by significant personal hardships, all of which have challenged her endurance and courage. Despite the difficulty, she has constantly shown incredible tenacity in overcoming challenges and pursuing her love for truth and justice. Here are some of the personal problems Christiane has faced and how she has demonstrated resilience:

Balancing profession and Family: Christiane has had a difficult time balancing the demands of her high-profile profession with her personal life and family obligations. Frequent travel, long hours, and exposure to tragic situations have damaged her relationships, forcing her to make difficult decisions between her job and her loved ones. Resilience: Christiane has addressed this issue with grace and tenacity, finding ways to make time for her family despite her hectic schedule and keeping open channels of contact with them. She has welcomed the support of her family and coworkers, relying on them for encouragement and assistance at difficult moments.

Emotional Toll of Reporting: Reporting from crisis zones and witnessing human suffering may be emotionally taxing for journalists like Christiane. The stress, trauma, and moral quandaries that come with her job have put her mental resilience and emotional well-being to the test. Resilience: Despite the emotional demands of her job, Christiane has shown amazing resilience in overcoming hardship and dealing with the psychological consequences of her experiences. She got treatment from mental health specialists, practiced self-care, and built a solid support network to help her navigate the emotional intricacies of her job.

Criticism and Controversy: As a prominent journalist, Christiane has encountered criticism and controversy throughout her career, ranging from claims of prejudice to scrutiny of her reporting methods and personal opinions. Dealing with public scrutiny and bad criticism may be emotionally draining and difficult to manage. Christiane has handled criticism with perseverance and grace, refusing to be distracted or misled from her dedication to journalistic ethics and truth-telling. She has viewed criticism as a chance for growth and introspection, taking input and applying it to improve her reporting and professional practices.

Christiane, like many others, has encountered health issues throughout her life and profession. These obstacles, whether physical or mental, can impair one's capacity to work and retain a sense of well-being. Christiane has faced health issues with perseverance and tenacity, seeking medical treatment and assistance as needed and prioritizing her well-being despite the demands of her work. She has seen health setbacks as transitory barriers that must be overcome, relying on her inner strength and tenacity to persevere in the face of adversity.

Chapter 7

Amanpour's Global Influence

INTERNATIONAL REACH AND IMPACT

Christiane Amanpour's journalistic influence transcends national lines, reaching audiences all around the world with her smart reporting, courageous journalism, and steadfast devotion to truth and justice. Here are some important features of her global reach and impact:

Christiane's reporting has reached millions of people throughout the world through her work with CNN, PBS, and other international news organizations. Her enthralling narrative and in-depth research have captivated audiences across nations and countries, creating better understanding and empathy among viewers from all backgrounds.

Christiane's multilingual proficiency, which includes English, Persian, and French, has allowed her to connect with audiences in other nations and speak with sources in their original languages. This language diversity allows her to establish relationships with interview subjects and traverse complicated cultural circumstances, resulting in more nuanced and effective reporting.

Christiane's services to journalism have been acknowledged with various accolades and distinctions on a worldwide scale, including Emmys, the Edward R. Murrow Award, and the Peabody Award. These awards recognize her impact and influence as a renowned voice in the global media environment.

Advocacy for Press Freedom: As a strong supporter of press freedom and human rights, Christiane has used her position to highlight challenges to media freedom and the suffering of journalists facing censorship, harassment, and violence all over the world. Her lobbying activities have increased awareness about the value of a free and independent press in preserving democracy and keeping authority accountable.

Christiane's reporting from conflict zones and humanitarian crises has had a direct influence on international events, influencing public opinion, driving policy debates, and stimulating action by governments and international organizations. Her articles have raised awareness about the condition of disadvantaged groups, sparked humanitarian responses, and helped to promote peace and justice in crisis zones.

Cultural Bridge Building: Christiane's work as a foreign reporter has acted as a cultural bridge between many countries and civilizations, encouraging greater understanding and discussion among varied people. Her ability to traverse complicated cultural dynamics and interact with varied viewpoints has aided in bridging gaps and promoting cross-cultural empathy and collaboration.

LEGACY AND INFLUENCE ON JOURNALISM

Christiane Amanpour's impact on journalism is significant and far-reaching, marked by her courageous search for the truth, unshakable dedication to journalistic integrity, and persistent fight for human rights and press freedom. Her impact on the field of journalism is evident, influencing the practices, viewpoints, and goals of journalists worldwide. Here are a few important aspects of her legacy and influence:

Christiane's groundbreaking career has pioneered the way for women in journalism, breaking down barriers and defying gender stereotypes in an industry dominated by males. Her accomplishments as a foreign reporter have motivated numerous women to seek careers in journalism and advance to top positions in media companies.

Fearless Reporting from Conflict Zones: Christiane's fearless reporting from conflict zones has established a new standard for brave journalism, demonstrating the power of narrative to bear testimony to the human cost of war and persecution. Her determination to go into dangerous situations and give voice to the unheard has inspired a new generation of journalists to face hardship with courage and conviction.

champion for Press Freedom and Human Rights: Christiane, a passionate champion for press freedom and human rights, has used her position to highlight challenges to media freedom as well as the suffering of journalists who face censorship, harassment, and violence. Her advocacy activities have rallied support for press freedom throughout the world, emphasizing the necessity of independent media in preserving democracy and holding authority accountable.

Christiane's reporting has had a long-term influence on international politics, influencing public opinion, driving policy debates, and stimulating action by governments and international organizations. Her reports from conflict zones and humanitarian crises have raised awareness of disadvantaged groups' predicament, sparked humanitarian responses, and helped to attempt to promote peace and justice in conflict situations.

An exemplar of Journalistic ethics: Throughout her career, Christiane has demonstrated the greatest levels of journalistic ethics and professionalism, garnering the respect and admiration of both colleagues and viewers. Her dedication to truth, impartiality, and empathy has established a standard for ethical journalism and motivated others to embrace the ideals of honesty and accountability in their work.

Inspiration for future generations: Christiane's legacy as a journalist and fighter for truth and justice will encourage future generations of journalists to pursue their love for storytelling, to confront injustice and oppression, and to make a good difference in the world via their work. Her lasting impact on the profession of journalism acts as a source of hope and inspiration for aspiring journalists all across the world.

Chapter 8

Criticism and Controversies

Ethical dilemmas and criticisms

Throughout her remarkable career, Christiane Amanpour has faced ethical quandaries and criticism, reflecting the complexities of journalism and the difficulties associated with reporting on sensitive and political matters. Here are some examples of ethical quandaries she has encountered and comments she has received:

Objectivity vs. Advocacy: Christiane has been criticized for blurring the distinction between objective reporting and advocacy journalism. While she strives for neutrality in her reporting, her strong support for human rights and press freedom has caused some to question her objectivity. The conflict between journalistic impartiality and advocacy for social justice is a recurrent ethical quandary for journalists reporting on global concerns.

Access to Sources: When reporting from authoritarian regimes and combat zones, journalists like Christiane frequently face severe ethical quandaries over source access. In some situations, obtaining access to sensitive information or interviews may necessitate violating journalistic values or making ethical sacrifices. Christiane must balance the dangers and implications of her actions while remaining committed to truth-telling and responsibility.

Conflict of Interest: Christiane has been chastised for potential conflicts of interest stemming from her ties with media groups and relationships with politicians and officials. Maintaining editorial independence and avoiding conflicts of interest is critical for retaining journalistic integrity and credibility, and Christiane must be watchful in preventing impressions of prejudice or undue influence.

Accuracy and Fact-Checking: In today's fast-paced world of 24-hour news coverage, journalists like Christiane must prioritize accuracy and comprehensive fact-checking. However, the temptation to break news rapidly and compete for ratings can occasionally result in mistakes or inaccuracies in reporting. Christiane has been chastised for inconsistencies in her reporting, emphasizing the significance of thorough fact-checking and adhering to journalistic norms.

Sensationalism and Trauma Coverage: Reporting on traumatic events and humanitarian crises raises ethical concerns about sensationalism and the potential to re-traumatize survivors. Christiane must strike a balance between the need to inform the public and respect for the experiences of people impacted by the tragedy. Critics may accuse journalists of exploiting human misery for ratings or sensationalizing events for dramatic effect, stressing the ethical quandaries inherent in trauma reporting.

Censorship and Government Interference: Journalists like Christiane who work in authoritarian regimes or conflict zones frequently suffer censorship, intimidation, and harassment from governments and other strong entities. Criticism of her reporting might originate from attempts to silence dissenting voices or control the narrative. Christiane must face these problems with fortitude and resilience, while committed to journalistic freedom and the public's right to know.

Chapter 9

BEYOND JOURNALISM

PHILANTHROPY AND HUMANITARIAN WORK

In addition to her remarkable journalism career, Christiane Amanpour has been an active philanthropist and humanitarian, using her platform and influence to work for social justice, human rights, and global development. Here are some instances of her charitable and humanitarian work:

Support for Press Freedom: Christiane is a strong supporter of press freedom and has participated in several projects aimed at safeguarding journalists and preserving the rights of free and independent media. She has spoken out against censorship, harassment, and violence against journalists throughout the world and has backed groups committed to advancing press freedom and protecting journalists' rights.

Humanitarian Reporting: Christiane's reporting from conflict zones and humanitarian crises has raised awareness of the condition of vulnerable populations, catalyzing humanitarian actions to alleviate suffering and promote peace. Her tales have raised awareness about topics like as displacement, refugee rights, and access to humanitarian relief, pushing viewers and policymakers to take action and show support.

Christiane is a strong supporter of women's rights and gender equality, and she uses her platform to spotlight the experiences and hardships of women and girls all over the world. She has written extensively about gender-based violence, access to education and healthcare, and women's empowerment, highlighting the voices of women leaders and activists fighting to promote gender equality.

Support for Refugee Causes: Christiane has been actively involved in promoting awareness and support for refugees and displaced people, highlighting the issues they confront and campaigning for legislation that protects their rights and dignity. She has worked with humanitarian groups to offer aid to refugees and lobby for a more humane and inclusive refugee policy.

Education and Empowerment: Christiane is a big supporter of education as a tool for social transformation and empowerment. She has supported educational projects focused on increasing access to excellent education for vulnerable people, particularly girls, and women, since she understands the transforming power of education on individuals and society.

Climate Change Advocacy: Christiane has been outspoken on the critical need to address climate change and environmental degradation, emphasizing the disproportionate impact of environmental problems on vulnerable people worldwide. She has utilized her position to increase environmental awareness and push for legislation that reduces the consequences of climate change while promoting sustainability.

CONCLUSION

Christiane Amanpour's incredible career as a journalist, advocate, and humanitarian has had an everlasting effect on the media landscape and beyond. Her fearless reporting from conflict zones, passionate advocacy for press freedom and human rights, and unwavering commitment to truth and integrity have inspired generations of journalists and viewers to confront injustice, challenge the status quo, and work for a more just and equitable world.

From her early days as a correspondent covering the Gulf War to her groundbreaking interviews with world leaders and the founding of "Amanpour & Company," Christiane has consistently pushed the boundaries of journalism, shedding light on today's most pressing issues and amplifying the voices of the marginalized and oppressed.

Beyond her professional accomplishments, Christiane's charitable and humanitarian efforts demonstrate her profound dedication to social justice, gender equality, refugee rights, education, and environmental sustainability. She has utilized her position to not just enlighten and educate, but also to push for good change and help those in need.

Printed in Great Britain
by Amazon